how2become

Scottish Police Tests
INFORMATION HANDLING

www.How2Become.com

by How2Become

Orders: Please contact How2Become Ltd, Suite 14, 50 Churchill Square Business Centre, Kings Hill, Kent ME19 4YU. You can also order via the email address info@How2Become.co.uk.

ISBN: 978-1910202289

First published in 2014 by How2Become Ltd

Typeset for How2Become Ltd by Anton Pshinka.

Printed in Great Britain for How2Become Ltd by Bell & Bain Ltd, 303 Burnfield Road, Thornliebank, Glasgow G46 7UQ.

Attend a 1 Day Police Officer Training Course by visiting:

www.PoliceCourse.co.uk

Get more products for passing Scottish Police selection at:

www.How2Become.com

CONTENTS

As part of this product you have received access to FREE online tests that will help you to pass the Scottish Police Tests!

To gain access, simply go to:

www.PsychometricTestsOnline.co.uk

INTRODUCTION TO YOUR NEW GUIDE

Welcome to Scottish Police Information Handling Tests: The ULTIMATE guide for helping you to pass the standard entrance test for the Scottish Police service. This guide has been designed to help you prepare for, and pass, the tough police officer selection process.

The selection process to join the police is highly competitive. Approximately 65,000 people apply to join the police every year. But what is even more staggering is that only approximately 7,000 of those applicants will be successful. You could view this as a worrying statistic, or alternatively you could view it that you are determined to be one of the 7,000 who are successful. Armed with this insider's guide, you have certainly taken the first step to passing the police officer selection process.

About the Scottish Police Standard Entrance Test

The test is made up of three papers. There are three different versions of the test, therefore all applicants are allowed to sit the Standard Entrance Test (SET) a maximum of three times. The test covers:

- language
- numbers
- information handling

To help you get ready for the test, we've created sample INFORMATION HANDLING test questions for you to practice.

Work through each test carefully before checking your answers at the end of the test.

There are plenty of test questions for you to try out within this guide which are relevant to the INFORMATION HANDLING test element of the selection process. Once you have completed the testing booklet you may wish to access our online police testing facility which you can find at:

www.How2Become.com

Don't ever give up on your dreams; if you really want to become a police officer, then you can do it. The way to approach the police officer selection process is to embark on a programme of 'in-depth' preparation and this guide will help you to do exactly that.

The police officer selection process is not easy to pass. Unless, that is, you put in plenty of preparation. Your preparation must be focused in the right areas, and also be comprehensive enough to give you every chance of success. This guide will teach you how to be a successful candidate.

The way to pass the police officer selection process is to develop your own skills and experiences around the core competencies that are required to become a police officer. Many candidates who apply to join the police will be unaware that the core competencies even exist. This guide has been specifically designed to help you prepare for the Police Initial Recruitment Test that forms part of the assessment centre.

If you need any further help with any element of the police officer selection process including role play, written test and interview, then we offer a wide range of products to assist you. These are all available through our online shop www.How2Become.com. We also run a 1-day intensive Police Officer Course. Details are available at the website:

www.PoliceCourse.co.uk

Once again, thank you for your custom and we wish you every success in your pursuit to becoming a police officer.

Work hard, stay focused and be what you want…

Best wishes,

The How2Become Team

BEGINNER

SECTION 1

INFORMATION HANDLING TEST EXERCISE 1

Study the graph carefully then answer questions 1 - 6

Shoplifting by month and location

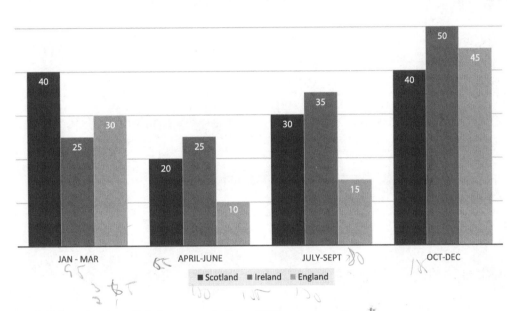

Q1. In which months did the most shoplifting occur?

ANSWER

Q2. In which location did the most shoplifting occur?

ANSWER

Q3. In total, how many shoplifting incidents happened between Jan-Mar?

ANSWER

Q4. In total, how many shoplifting incidents happened in England?

ANSWER

Q5. From January to December, how many shoplifting incidents occurred in Scotland?

ANSWER

Q6. How many shoplifting incidents were there in total?

ANSWER

INFORMATION HANDLING TEST EXERCISE 2

Study the graph carefully then answer questions 1 – 6

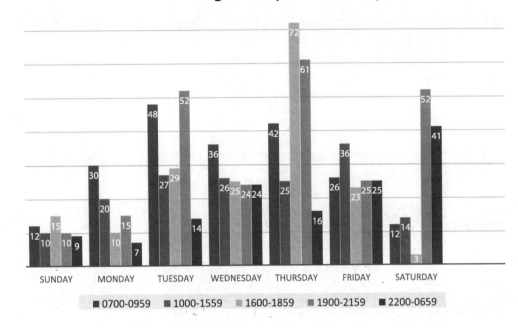

No. of burglaries by time and day

Q1. What day of the week are most burglaries committed?

ANSWER

Q2. On what day are burglaries least likely to be committed?

ANSWER

Q3. How many burglaries are committed on Friday between 10:00 – 15:59?

ANSWER [   ]

Q4. On what day and between what times are burglaries mostly committed?

ANSWER [   ]

Q5. How many burglaries are committed in total between the hours of 07:00 and 09:59?

ANSWER [   ]

Q6. How many burglaries were committed in total?

ANSWER [   ]

INFORMATION HANDLING TEST EXERCISE 3

Study the graph carefully then answer questions 1 - 6

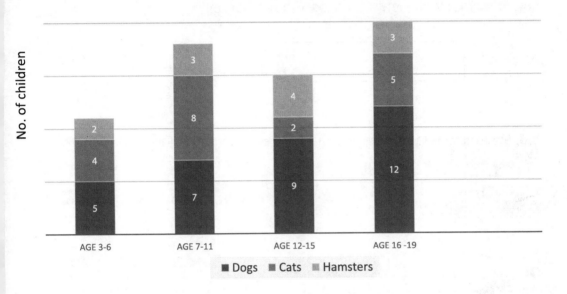

Children's favourite animals

Q1. What is the most popular animal between the ages of 7 and 11?

ANSWER

Q2. Amongst all ages, how many children chose cats as their favourite animal?

ANSWER

Q3. Which age group was hamsters least popular with?

ANSWER [   ]

Q4. How many students took part in the survey?

ANSWER [   ]

Q5. What is the least popular animal between the ages of 12 and 15?

ANSWER [   ]

Q6. What animal was most popular?

ANSWER [   ]

INFORMATION HANDLING TEST EXERCISE 4

Study the graph carefully then answer questions 1 - 6

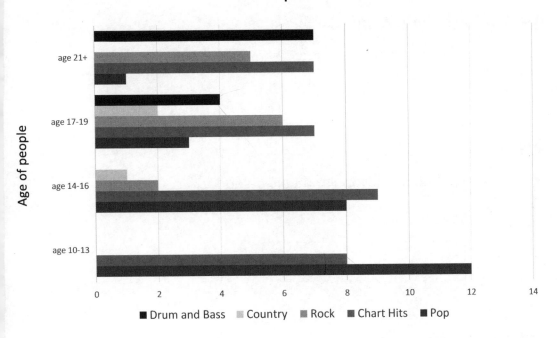

Music preferences

Q1. What was the most popular music choice between the ages of 14 and 16?

ANSWER

Q2. How many people liked country music?

ANSWER

Q3. In total, how many people liked drum and bass music?

ANSWER

Q4. What was the least popular music category?

ANSWER

Q5. What was the most popular music category?

ANSWER

Q6. Between the ages of 10 and 16, how many people liked chart hit music?

ANSWER

INFORMATION HANDLING TEST EXERCISE 5

Study the graph carefully then answer questions 1 - 6

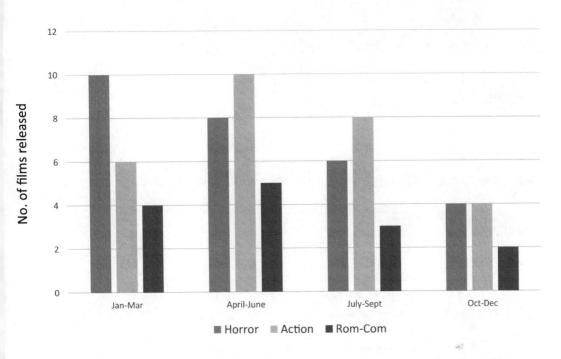

No. of films released and the genre

Q1. What was the most popular film genre between the months of July and September?

ANSWER

Q2. Over the 12 month period, what genre was released the least?

ANSWER

Q3. How many action films were released between January and September?

ANSWER

Q4. How many rom-com films were released in total?

ANSWER

Q5. How many films were released between April and June?

ANSWER

Q6. How many films were released in that 12 month period?

ANSWER

INFORMATION HANDLING TEST EXERCISE 6

Study the graph carefully then answer questions 1 - 6

Types of crimes committed in a 12 month period

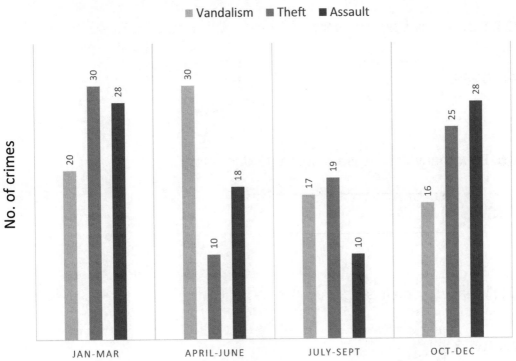

Q1. Between January and March, how many crimes were committed in total?

ANSWER

Q2. How many crimes were committed between April and June?

ANSWER

Q3. In total, how many crimes committed were vandalism?

ANSWER

Q4. How many assaults were there between January and September?

ANSWER

Q5. How many crimes were committed in total?

ANSWER

Q6. What was the least popular crime?

ANSWER

INFORMATION HANDLING TEST EXERCISE 7

Study the graph carefully then answer questions 1 - 6

Olympic sports and the number of viewers in that year

■ Cycling   ■ Football   ■ Tennis   ▦ Snowboarding   ■ Ice Hockey   ■ Ice Skating

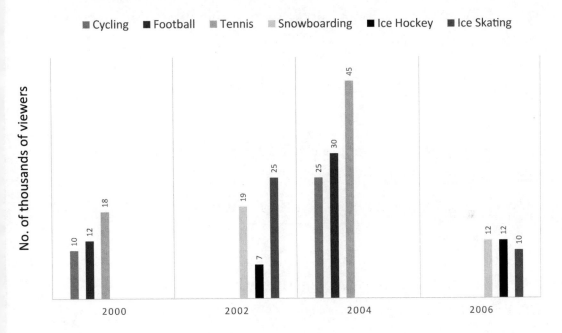

Q1. What was the most popular sport viewed in 2004?

ANSWER

Q2. How many people viewed tennis in 2000 and 2004?

ANSWER

Q3. What was the most popular sport viewed?

ANSWER

Q4. In total, how many more people preferred football over ice hockey?

ANSWER

Q5. In 2000, how many people viewed cycling, football and tennis?

ANSWER

Q6. What was the least viewed sport to watch?

ANSWER

INFORMATION HANDLING TEST EXERCISE 8

Study the graph carefully then answer questions 1 - 6

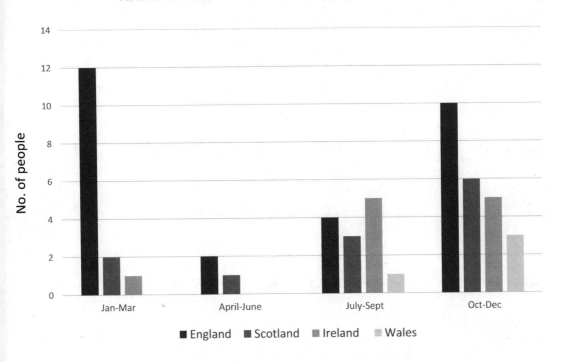

Knife crime in terms of month and location

Q1. What location has the most knife crimes over the 12 month period?

ANSWER

Q2. How many knife crimes were there between July and September?

ANSWER

Q3. What location had the least number of knife crimes?

ANSWER

Q4. Between April and December, how many knife crimes occurred in England and Scotland?

ANSWER

Q5. How many knife crimes happened in Ireland?

ANSWER

Q6. How many knife crimes occurred in all locations in the 12 month period?

ANSWER

INFORMATION HANDLING TEST EXERCISE 9

Study the graph carefully then answer questions 1 - 6

No. of users of Facebook based on age and sexuality in the UK

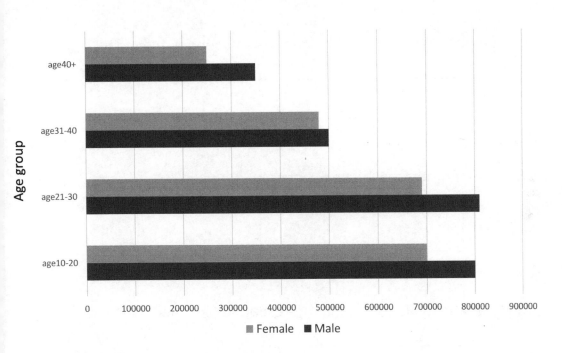

Q1. What was the most popular age group to use Facebook?

ANSWER

Q2. What is the difference between the number of males aged 10 to 20 and the number of males aged 31 to 40, who use Facebook?

ANSWER

Q3. How many females between the age of 10 and 20 use Facebook?

ANSWER

Q4. Between men and women, who used Facebook the most?

ANSWER

Q5. How many aged 40+ use Facebook?

ANSWER

Q6. What was the least popular age group to use Facebook?

ANSWER

INFORMATION HANDLING TEST EXERCISE 10

Study the graph carefully then answer questions 1 - 6

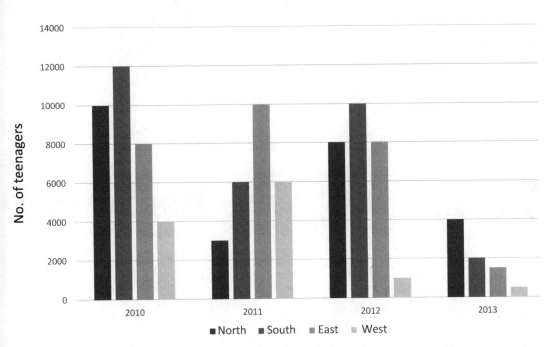

No. of teenage pregnancies in the UK

Q1. What location in the UK held the most teenage pregnancies in 2012?

ANSWER

Q2. How many teenage pregnancies did the North of the UK have in total?

ANSWER

Q3. What location in the UK has the most teenage pregnancies in total?

ANSWER

Q4. What location in the UK has the least number of teenage pregnancies in total?

ANSWER

Q5. In 2011 and 2013, how many teenage pregnancies happened in the South of the UK?

ANSWER

Q6. How many teenage pregnancies in total happened in 2010?

ANSWER

ANSWERS TO INFORMATION HANDLING BEGINNER (SECTION 1)

ANSWERS TO INFORMATION HANDLING TEST EXERCISE 1

Q1. Oct-Dec

Q2. Ireland

Q3. 95

Q4. 100

Q5. 130

Q6. 365

ANSWERS TO INFORMATION HANDLING TEST EXERCISE 2

Q1. Thursday

Q2. Sunday

Q3. 36

Q4. Thursday between the hours of 1600 and 1859

Q5. 206

Q6. 916

ANSWERS TO INFORMATION HANDLING TEST EXERCISE 3

Q1. Cats

Q2. 19

Q3. 3-6

Q4. 64

Q5. Cats

Q6. Dogs

ANSWERS TO INFORMATION HANDLING TEST EXERCISE 4

Q1. Chart hit

Q2. 3

Q3. 11

Q4. Country

Q5. Chart hit

Q6. 17

ANSWERS TO INFORMATION HANDLING TEST EXERCISE 5

Q1. Action

Q2. Rom-com

Q3. 24

Q4. 14

Q5. 23

Q6. 70

ANSWERS TO INFORMATION HANDLING TEST EXERCISE 6

Q1. 78

Q2. 58

Q3. 83

Q4. 56

Q5. 251

Q6. Vandalism

ANSWERS TO INFORMATION HANDLING TEST EXERCISE 7

Q1. Tennis

Q2. 63,000

Q3. Tennis

Q4. 23,000

Q5. 40,000

Q6. Ice Hockey

ANSWERS TO INFORMATION HANDLING TEST EXERCISE 8

Q1. England

Q2. 13

Q3. Wales

Q4. 26

Q5. 11

Q6. 55

ANSWERS TO INFORMATION HANDLING TEST EXERCISE 9

Q1. Between 10-20 and 21-30

Q2. 300,000

Q3. 700,000

Q4. Men

Q5. 600000

Q6. Age 40+

ANSWERS TO INFORMATION HANDLING TEST EXERCISE 10

Q1. South

Q2. 25000

Q3. South

Q4. West

Q5. 8000

Q6. 34000

BEGINNER

SECTION 2

INFORMATION HANDLING TEST EXERCISE 1

Study the table carefully then answer questions 1 - 6

Users of drugs and other intoxications between the ages of 16-25 living in the UK

	First time user	Constant user	Drug dealer	No use	User total:
Alcohol	30	50	-	5	80
Cigarettes	58	60	-	28	118
Cannabis	37	14	2	31	53
Ecstasy	20	21	1	19	42
Heroin	8	5	2	20	15
Cocaine	6	3	1	31	10
Other	3	1	1	-	5

Q1. If someone was a first time user, what are they most likely to use?

ANSWER

Q2. What is the most common type/s of drug for drug dealers to use?

ANSWER

Q3. In total, how many people used ecstasy?

ANSWER

Q4. How many constant users use cannabis, ecstasy and cigarettes as intoxicating products?

ANSWER

Q5. How many non-users are there for heroin and cocaine?

ANSWER

Q6. In total, how many people used or sells any of these drug or intoxicating products?

ANSWER

INFORMATION HANDLING TEST EXERCISE 2

Study the table carefully then answer questions 1 - 6

Serious criminology and the type of sentence given

	Discharged	Serve minimum sentence	Long term Sentence	Reprimand	Other
Murder	1	10	15	0	1
Manslaughter	1	12	13	1	0
Infanticide	2	28	28	2	0
Kidnapping	1	12	8	4	1
Arson	4	13	12	1	0
Armed Robbery	6	24	2	1	1
Other	1	3	4	2	1

Q1. How many people served a minimum sentence for armed robbery?

ANSWER

Q2. What criminal offence gave the most long term sentences?

ANSWER

Q3. How many people were discharged for manslaughter?

ANSWER

Q4. What sentence was given the most for kidnapping?

ANSWER

Q5. For all criminal offences, how many people were to face a long term sentence?

ANSWER

Q6. For arson, how many people were either discharged or given a reprimand for their criminal activity?

ANSWER

INFORMATION HANDLING TEST EXERCISE 3

Study the table carefully then answer questions 1 - 6

Types of offences and type of sentence

	Discharge	Fine	Community service	Suspended sentence	Custodial sentence	Other
Drug offences	12	18	16	1	9	1
Theft	10	13	3	14	10	3
Criminal damage	31	8	31	14	10	4
Sexual offence	41	13	4	19	31	1
Motoring	13	51	31	21	11	4
Bodily harm	10	10	41	21	32	-

Q1. If someone has been convicted of bodily harm, what is the sentence that they are most likely to receive?

ANSWER

Q2. Which offence is least likely to get a custodial sentence?

ANSWER

Q3. Which offence is most likely to get a fine?

ANSWER

Q4. What is the most common sentence for theft?

ANSWER
[   ]

Q5. In total, how many people were charged with a custodial sentence for criminal damage?

ANSWER
[   ]

Q6. In total, how many people were charged with either a custodial or suspended sentence for drug offences?

ANSWER
[   ]

INFORMATION HANDLING TEST EXERCISE 4

Study the table carefully then answer questions 1 - 6

Favourite sports in regards to age

	10-19	20-29	30-39	40-49	50-59	60+
Football	100	59	54	49	23	10
Dance	86	68	25	12	13	16
Tennis	79	76	46	25	36	46
Golf	13	16	20	13	69	64
Hockey	12	31	21	10	6	1
Gymnastics	10	16	10	8	4	-

Q1. Between the age of 30 and 39, what is the most viewed sport?

ANSWER

Q2. In total, how many people view football?

ANSWER

Q3. Which sport is the most popular across all ages?

ANSWER

Q4. Which sport is the least popular between the ages of 10 and 19?

ANSWER

Q5. In total, how many people view gymnastics?

ANSWER

Q6. What age group watches the least amount of sport?

ANSWER

INFORMATION HANDLING TEST EXERCISE 5

Study the table carefully then answer questions 1 - 6

Preference of animal in regards to age

	10-19	20-29	30-39	40-49	50-59	60+
Dogs	45	36	20	12	35	13
Cats	35	12	8	12	10	6
Hamsters	12	6	14	1	-	-
Goldfish	42	36	14	36	12	10
Birds	10	12	6	2	1	6

Q1. What age group prefers goldfish?

ANSWER

Q2. How many people prefer dogs?

ANSWER

Q3. If you were aged 35, which animal are you least likely to get?

ANSWER

Q4. If you were aged 62, what animal are you most likely to get?

ANSWER

[   ]

Q5. How many more people prefer dogs than cats?

ANSWER

[   ]

Q6. In total, how many people prefer hamsters?

ANSWER

[   ]

INFORMATION HANDLING TEST EXERCISE 6

Study the table carefully then answer questions 1 - 6

Favourite holiday destinations in terms of age

	Spain	Australia	America	Mexico	Ireland	Tenerife	Italy	In total:
Age18-29	45	10	25	9	12	36	30	167
Age30-39	28	12	31	35	27	10	27	170
Age40-49	8	10	17	3	64	4	31	137
Age50+	3	47	21	1	30	-	17	119

Q1. If you were to go to Tenerife, between what age are you most likely to go?

ANSWER

Q2. If you were 38 years old, where are you least likely to go on holiday?

ANSWER

Q3. How many people go to Mexico between the ages of 40 and 49?

ANSWER

Q4. What is the most popular holiday destination?

ANSWER

Q5. What is the least favourite holiday destination?

ANSWER

Q6. How many people went to America between the ages of 18 and 29 and 40 and 49?

ANSWER

INFORMATION HANDLING TEST EXERCISE 7

Study the table carefully then answer questions 1 - 6

Teenage delinquency and deviant behaviour in regards to location in the UK in 2012

	England	Scotland	Ireland	Wales	In total:
Teenage Pregnancy	102	56	36	10	204
ASB	69	49	38	67	223
Drug use	58	69	42	16	185
Alcohol abuse	69	48	59	36	212
Vandalism	45	49	69	15	178

Q1. If you lived in England, what teenage problem are you most likely to face?

ANSWER

Q2. If you lived in Wales, what teenage problem are you least likely to face?

ANSWER

Q3. How many teenage pregnancies occurred in the UK in 2012?

ANSWER

Q4. What teenage problem is the most problematic?

ANSWER [   ]

Q5. In Scotland, how many teenage problems were there in 2012?

ANSWER [   ]

Q6. In total, across the UK, how many teenage problems did the UK face in 2012?

ANSWER [   ]

INFORMATION HANDLING TEST EXERCISE 8

Study the table carefully then answer questions 1 - 6

GCSE grade results of a local Secondary School

	A	B	C	D	E	U	Total Pass	Total Fails
Maths	8	22	46	10	3	4	89	4
English	10	7	35	15	15	11	82	11
Science	6	19	28	23	10	7	86	7
Technology	21	15	40	15	1	1	92	1
Geography	6	16	34	27	6	4	89	4
History	16	6	43	16	7	5	88	5

Q1. Across all subjects, how many passes did the school get for their GCSE's?

ANSWER

Q2. What subject got the most number of A's?

ANSWER

Q3. What subject got the most C's?

ANSWER

Q4. How many U grades did Technology get?

ANSWER

Q5. How many students took part in the survey?

ANSWER

Q6. What subject received 23 D grades?

ANSWER

INFORMATION HANDLING TEST EXERCISE 9

Study the table carefully then answer questions 1 - 6

Number of films released yearly based on the genre of the film

	2000	2001	2002	2003	2004	2005	2006
Horror	6	2	5	9	4	3	2
Romance	4	3	1	5	6	3	4
Comedy	4	3	5	1	6	4	3
Action	4	2	3	6	5	4	3
Drama	1	2	1	-	-	3	2
Total:	19	12	15	21	21	17	14

Q1. How many films were released in 2002?

ANSWER

Q2. What was the most popular genre in 2003?

ANSWER

Q3. Between 2000 and 2006, how many romance films have been released?

ANSWER

Q4. What genre had 6 films released in 2003?

ANSWER

Q5. What is the most released genre since 2000 to 2006?

ANSWER

Q6. What genre was least released in 2005?

ANSWER

INFORMATION HANDLING TEST EXERCISE 10

Study the table carefully then answer questions 1 - 6

Favourite leisure activity in terms of age

	Age10-19	20-29	30-39	40-49	50+
Dancing	100	30	25	15	5
Football	80	80	20	10	10
Reading	75	25	25	25	50
TV	75	75	30	10	10
Sleeping	30	50	40	30	40

Q1. What leisure activity is most popular between the ages of 50+?

ANSWER

Q2. What leisure activity is least popular between the ages of 10-19?

ANSWER

Q3. If you were 27, what leisure activity are you most likely to enjoy?

ANSWER

Q4. If you were 39, what leisure activity are you least likely to enjoy?

ANSWER

Q5. How many people enjoy reading?

ANSWER

Q6. How many more people like sleeping than dancing between the ages of 30-39?

ANSWER

ANSWERS TO INFORMATION HANDLING BEGINNER (SECTION 2)

ANSWERS TO INFORMATION HANDLING TEST EXERCISE 1

Q1. Cigarettes

Q2. Cannabis and heroin

Q3. 42

Q4. 95

Q5. 51

Q5. 323

ANSWERS TO INFORMATION HANDLING TEST EXERCISE 2

Q1. 24

Q2. Infanticide

Q3. 1

Q4. Serve minimum sentence

Q5. 82

Q6. 5

ANSWERS TO INFORMATION HANDLING TEST EXERCISE 3

Q1. Community service

Q2. Drug offences

Q3. Motoring

Q4. Suspended sentence

Q5. 10

Q6. 10

ANSWERS TO INFORMATION HANDLING TEST EXERCISE 4

Q1. Football

Q2. 295

Q3. Tennis

Q4. Gymnastics

Q5. 48

Q6. 40-49

ANSWERS TO INFORMATION HANDLING TEST EXERCISE 5

Q1. 10-19

Q2. 161

Q3. Bird

Q4. Dog

Q5. 78

Q6. 33

ANSWERS TO INFORMATION HANDLING TEST EXERCISE 6

Q1. 18-29

Q2. Tenerife

Q3. 3

Q4. Ireland

Q5. Mexico

Q6. 42

ANSWERS TO INFORMATION HANDLING TEST EXERCISE 7

Q1. Teenage pregnancy

Q2. Teenage pregnancy

Q3. 204

Q4. Anti-social behaviour

Q5. 271

Q6. 1,002

ANSWERS TO INFORMATION HANDLING TEST EXERCISE 8

Q1. 526

Q2. Technology

Q3. Maths

Q4. 1

Q5. 93

Q6. Science

ANSWERS TO INFORMATION HANDLING TEST EXERCISE 9

Q1. 15

Q2. Horror

Q3. 26

Q4. Action

Q5. Horror

Q6. Horror, romance and drama

ANSWERS TO INFORMATION HANDLING TEST EXERCISE 10

Q1. Reading

Q2. Sleeping

Q3. Football

Q4. Football

Q5. 200

Q6. 15

INTERMEDIATE

SECTION 1

INFORMATION HANDLING TEST EXERCISE 1

Study the table carefully then answer questions 1 - 6

	After students leave school...	
	Male	Female
College	15000	10000
University	26000	45621
Apprenticeship	9000	1236
Job	8523	6354
Total =	58523	63211

Q1. How many people will be going to university?

ANSWER

Q2. How many females will get a job after leaving school?

ANSWER

Q3. How many more females than males will go to university?

ANSWER

Q4. In total, how many people will get an apprenticeship after leaving school?

ANSWER

Q5. If you were female and leaving school, what are you most likely to do?

ANSWER

Q6. If you were male and leaving school, what are you least likely to do?

ANSWER

INFORMATION HANDLING TEST EXERCISE 2

Study the table carefully then answer questions 1 - 6

Type of establishment	Secondary School		University	
	Male	Female	Male	Female
Football	256	62	398	162
Dance	165	268	169	368
Boxing	13	3	358	123
Tennis	98	68	160	76
Rounders	16	68	26	43
Total =	548	469	1111	772

Football = 878
Dance = 970
Boxing = 497
Tennis = 402
Rounders = 153

Q1. What was the most popular sport?

ANSWER [   ]

Q2. How many more people played boxing in university compared to secondary school?

ANSWER [   ]

Q3. If you were male, and you were heading to university, what is the most likely sport you will play?

ANSWER

Q4. In total, how many people enjoyed the game of rounders?

ANSWER

Q5. How many females enjoyed playing tennis?

ANSWER

Q6. In total, how many university students enjoyed playing any type of sport?

ANSWER

INFORMATION HANDLING TEST EXERCISE 3

Study the table carefully then answer questions 1 - 6

Holiday Preferences	Abroad				In the UK			
	Spain		America		Butlins		Lake District	
	Couples	Family	Couples	Family	Couples	Family	Couples	Family
All inclusive	103	208	287	316	12	176	68	109
Half board	216	233	187	84	6	164	52	68
Self Service	36	95	79	65	1	76	36	49
Total =	355	536	553	465	19	416	156	226

Total no. holidays = 2726

All inclusive = 1279
Half Board = 1010
Self Service = 437

Q1. In total, how many all-inclusive holidays were there?

ANSWER

Q2. If you were to go away abroad as a family, where are you most likely to go?

ANSWER

Q3. How many half board holidays were there in that year?

ANSWER

Q4. If you were in a couple, are you more likely to go abroad or somewhere in the UK?

ANSWER

Q5. If you booked an all-inclusive holiday for your family in the UK, where are you most likely to go?

ANSWER

Q6. Which holiday destination proves to be most popular?

ANSWER

INFORMATION HANDLING TEST EXERCISE 4

Study the table carefully then answer questions 1 - 6

Type of establishment	Non-Indictable Offences								Indictable Offences							
	Male				Female				Male				Female			
	Convicted		Awaiting trial		Convicted		Awaiting trial		Convicted		Awaiting trial		Convicted		Awaiting trial	
	A	U21	A	U21	A	U21	A	U21	A	U21	A	U21	A	U21	A	U21
Prison	485	180	68	52	153	35	12	19	208	189	12	16	96	103	7	19
Youth institutions		86		16		73		69		64		15		52		36
Total:	485	266	68	68	153	108	12	88	208	253	12	31	96	155	7	55

A = Adults
U21 – Under 21

Grand total = 2065

Prison = 1654
Youth Institutions = 411

Male = 1391
Female = 674

Q1. How many convicted young men aged under 21 are in prison for any type of offence?

ANSWER

Q2. In total, how many aged under 21 are in youth institutions?

ANSWER

Q3. How many adults are awaiting trial for non-indictable offences?

ANSWER

Q4. How many females are awaiting trial?

ANSWER

Q5. How many male adults, who are convicted prisoners, are there in total?

ANSWER

Q6. How many more people are in prison as opposed to youth institutions?

ANSWER

INFORMATION HANDLING TEST EXERCISE 5

Study the table carefully then answer questions 1 - 6

	Convicted				Non - Convicted			
	Male		Female		Male		Female	
	A	U21	A	U21	A	U21	A	U21
Theft	166	265	68	96	46	26	24	15
Drug Offences	356	254	126	85	12	4	4	3
Motoring	369	369	49	109	56	65	31	45
Criminal Damage	256	251	169	56	43	15	2	13
Sexual Offences	235	96	19	10	5	3	2	1
Fraud	357	23	120	8	13	11	16	10
Total =	1739	1258	551	364	175	124	79	87

Grand Total = 4377

Convictions = 3912
Non Convictions = 465

Q1. In total, how many convictions were there for drug offences?

ANSWER

Q2. How many non-convictions were there for motoring offences aged under 21?

ANSWER

Q3. How many convictions were there in total for male adults?

ANSWER

Q4. If you were aged under 21 and female, what is the most likely offence that you will be convicted for?

ANSWER

Q5. In total, how many fraud offences occurred by adults?

ANSWER

Q6. How many more convictions were there as opposed to non-convicted offences?

ANSWER

INFORMATION HANDLING TEST EXERCISE 6

Study the table carefully then answer questions 1 - 6

Job Occupation	England		Scotland		Ireland		Wales	
	Male	Female	Male	Female	Male	Female	Male	Female
Police officer	165	251	150	76	30	26	45	13
Teacher	98	208	96	120	23	64	36	65
Musician	206	121	126	35	169	13	76	9
Doctor	365	68	43	35	46	26	16	15
Sales	156	65	56	32	54	18	62	36
Total =	990	713	471	298	322	147	235	138

Grand Total = 3314

No. of Police officers = 756
No. of Teachers = 710
No. of Musicians = 755
No. of Doctors = 614
No. of Sales = 479

Q1. If you were male and lived in Scotland, what job are you most likely to have?

ANSWER

Q2. How many police officers are there across England and Scotland?

ANSWER

Q3. 126 males have what profession?

ANSWER

Q4. In total, how many people are in sales?

ANSWER

Q5. How many females have the job as a teacher?

ANSWER

Q6. What was the grand total of this survey?

ANSWER

INFORMATION HANDLING TEST EXERCISE 7

Study the table carefully then answer questions 1 - 6

Drug Use	England				Scotland			
	Male		Female		Male		Female	
	A	U21	A	U21	A	U21	A	U21
Cannabis	358	165	163	113	132	76	45	33
Heroin	153	75	76	65	103	56	16	12
Cocaine	136	16	131	35	86	35	11	9
Other	56	35	32	12	32	12	9	6
	703	291	402	225	353	179	81	60

Total Drug Use: 2294

Cannabis = 1085
Heroin = 556
Cocaine = 459
Other = 194

Q1. How many people used drugs in total?

ANSWER

Q2. What location proves less likely to take drugs?

ANSWER

Q3. How many people used heroin in England?

ANSWER [ ]

Q4. In England and Scotland, how many used cocaine?

ANSWER [ ]

Q5. What drug was most popular to use if England in you were under 21 and female?

ANSWER [ ]

Q6. What drug was most popular to use in Scotland if you were an adult and male?

ANSWER [ ]

INFORMATION HANDLING TEST EXERCISE 8

Study the table carefully then answer questions 1 - 6

Intoxication	Alcohol		Cigarettes	
	Male	Female	Male	Female
Recommended	12	63	-	-
2-3 (units/per)	36	23	26	36
4-5 (units/per)	49	36	64	45
5+	56	26	59	32
Total =	153	148	149	113

Q1. In total, how many people drink alcohol?

ANSWER

Q2. How many females have cigarettes?

ANSWER

Q3. In total, how many men drink 4-5 units of alcohol?

ANSWER

Q4. In total, how many women smoke 4-5 cigarettes?

ANSWER

Q5. How many people in total use cigarettes and/or alcohol?

ANSWER

Q6. For females, what is the most likely amount they would drink in regards to alcohol?

ANSWER

INFORMATION HANDLING TEST EXERCISE 9

Study the table carefully then answer questions 1 - 6

| location | Teenage pregnancy regarding location in the UK | | | | | | | |
| | England | | Scotland | | Ireland | | Wales | |
	13-16	17-20	13-16	17-20	13-16	17-20	13-16	17-20
Keeping the baby	36	63	11	23	19	23	2	3
Abortion	12	13	6	13	16	3	0	1
Adoption	16	16	8	9	4	5	1	1
Undecided	43	23	16	11	18	19	1	2
Total =	107	115	41	56	57	50	4	7

Total no. pregnancies = 437

England = 222
Scotland = 97
Ireland = 107
Wales = 11

Q1. Where would you be living in order to have the least chance of teenage pregnancy?

ANSWER

Q2. What location has the highest level of teenage pregnancy?

ANSWER

Q3. How many people in the survey wanted to keep their baby from England and Ireland?

ANSWER

Q4. In total, how many people wanted to give their baby up for adoption?

ANSWER

Q5. If you were living in Ireland, at what age group are you most likely to get pregnant?

ANSWER

Q6. How many people living in England wanted to keep their baby?

ANSWER

INFORMATION HANDLING TEST EXERCISE 10

Study the table carefully then answer questions 1 - 6

	Male				Female			
	18-25	26-35	36-49	50+	18-25	26-35	36-49	50+
Toyota	103	196	186	276	265	268	168	150
Ford	206	186	275	46	356	268	163	96
Mercedes	23	96	68	196	2	23	68	42
Renault	352	172	165	23	67	154	86	41
BMW	12	32	68	146	3	35	76	32
Vauxhall	269	126	112	136	109	120	162	106
Other	5	8	13	21	3	23	32	36
Total =	970	816	887	844	805	891	755	503

Grand total = 6471

Q1. If you were a 23 year old female, what car are you most likely to get?

ANSWER

Q2. What car is the most popular with men?

ANSWER

Q3. How many 18-25 year olds have a Ford?

ANSWER

Q4. What car (excluding 'Other') is least popular with females?

ANSWER

Q5. How many 26-35's have a car?

ANSWER

Q6. If you were a 50 year old man, what car are you most likely to have?

ANSWER

ANSWERS TO INFORMATION HANDLING INTERMEDIATE (SECTION 1)

ANSWERS TO INFORMATION HANDLING TEST EXERCISE 1

Q1. 71621

Q2. 6354

Q3. 19621

Q4. 10236

Q5. University

Q6. Job

ANSWERS TO INFORMATION HANDLING TEST EXERCISE 2

Q1. Dance

Q2. 465

Q3. Football

Q4. 153

Q5. 144

Q6. 1883

ANSWERS TO INFORMATION HANDLING TEST EXERCISE 3

Q1. 1279

Q2. Spain

Q3. 1010

Q4. Abroad

Q5. Butlins

Q6. America

ANSWERS TO INFORMATION HANDLING TEST EXERCISE 4

Q1. 369

Q2. 411

Q3. 80

Q4. 162

Q5. 693

Q6. 1243

ANSWERS TO INFORMATION HANDLING TEST EXERCISE 5

Q1. 821

Q2. 110

Q3. 1739

Q4. Motoring

Q5. 506

Q6. 3447

ANSWERS TO INFORMATION HANDLING TEST EXERCISE 6

Q1. Police officer

Q2. 642

Q3. Musician

Q4. 479

Q5. 457

Q6. 3314

ANSWERS TO INFORMATION HANDLING TEST EXERCISE 7

Q1. 2294

Q2. Scotland

Q3. 369

Q4. 459

Q5. Cannabis

Q6. Cannabis

ANSWERS TO INFORMATION HANDLING TEST EXERCISE 8

Q1. 301

Q2. 113

Q3. 49

Q4. 45

Q5. 563

Q6. The recommended amount

ANSWERS TO INFORMATION HANDLING TEST EXERCISE 9

Q1. Wales

Q2. England

Q3. 141

Q4. 60

Q5. 13-16

Q6. 99

ANSWERS TO INFORMATION HANDLING TEST EXERCISE 10

Q1. Ford

Q2. Toyota

Q3. 562

Q4. Mercedes

Q5. 1707

Q6. Toyota

INTERMEDIATE
SECTION 2

INFORMATION HANDLING TEST EXERCISE 1

Study the information in the list below. The following is an extract from the catalogue of books on sale at a book shop.

Catalogue page for books

Code 123: Youth Studies; Blackman, R. Paperback. £24.99 ISBN 0-3658-4532

Code 124: Introduction to youth culture; Downey, T. [download] £18.99 ISBN 0-4698- 6983

Code 125: Youth culture; Walker, P. Paperback. £27.99 ISBN 0-1355-4384

Code 126: Youth culture and Deviance; Downey, R. Hardback. £38.99 ISBN 0-9534-4381

Code 127: Youth and subcultures; Lewis, T. Hardback. £26.99 ISBN 0-9647-2535

Code 128: Youth – stereotypes and subcultures; Franklin, J. Hardback. £37.99 ISBN 0- 3258-7216

Code 129: The problematic youth of today; Johnson, M. Paperback. £27.99 ISBN 0-6589- 1234

Code 130: Theories of youth culture; Davidson, H. Hardback. £15.50 ISBN 0-7693-3586

Code 131: Understanding contemporary youth; Michaels, D. Hardback. £12.99 ISBN 0- 3635-6521

Code 132: Understanding contemporary youth in modern society; Michaels, D. Hardback. £18.99ISBN 0-3635-6522

Complete the missing entries in this customer order list

Entry Code	Price	Title	Author	Binding	ISBN
127		Youth and subcultures		Hardback	
	£15.50			Hardback	0-7693-3586
131			Michaels, D		0-3635-6521
	£24.99	Youth Studies			
124			Downey, T	[download]	

INFORMATION HANDLING TEST EXERCISE 2

Study the information in the list below. The following is an extract from the catalogue on a clothing website.

Catalogue on a clothing website

Code 110: Sophie May Backless Dress. White/Black. Size 10. £45.00 Ref no: 2569873

Code 111: Lilly Rose Sequinned Dress. Pink/ Black. Size 8. £25.99 Ref no: 4567823

Code 112: Summer Backless Prom Dress. Aqua. Size 12. £20.00 Ref no. 4258793

Code 113: Hannah May Long Sleeved Dress. Red. Size 12. £20.00 Ref no. 4632895

Code 114: Rosie Jane Bodycon Dress. Pink. Size 10. £10.00 Ref no. 7456325

Code 115: Fitted Alter neck Dress. Flowery. Size 6. £15.00 Ref no. 4796258

Code 116: Lucy May Maxi Dress. Blue/Silver. Size 8. £16.99 Ref no. 7432686

Code 117: Tailor made strapless dress. Black. Size 10. £9.99 Ref no. 1236852

Code 118: Juliette swirl Bodycon dress. Green. Size 12. £12.99 Ref no, 9635423

Complete the missing entries in this customer order list

Code	Name	Colour	Size	Price	Ref No.
Code 110		White/black			
	Summer backless prom dress			£20.00	
Code 114			10		7456325
	Tailor made strapless dress	Black			
				£12.99	9635423

INFORMATION HANDLING TEST EXERCISE 3

Study the information in the list below. The following is an extract from an Avon Book catalogue.

Avon Book Catalogue

Item 16:   Avon Black Mascara. Black. £5.99. Ref no. 14563259. pg. 5

Item 19:   Shimmery Lip gloss. Peach. £3.99. Ref no. 45339521. pg. 7

Item 20:   Shimmery Lip gloss. Pink. £3.99. Ref no. 45339522. pg. 7

Item 21:   Shimmery Lip gloss. Clear. £3.99. Ref no. 45339523. pg. 7

Item 25:   Shine and Clear Powder. Translucent. £3.99. Ref no. 56985326.
           pg. 9

Item 32:   Bristled foundation brush. £11.99. Ref no. 45692369. pg. 12

Item 33:   Powder Brush. £15.99. Ref no. 46691238. pg. 12

Item 38:   NEW! Magic Eyeliner. Black. £8.99. Ref no. 49684532. pg. 14

Item 39:   NEW! Magic Eyeliner. Brown. £8.99. Ref no. 49684533. pg. 14

Item 40:   Shimmery Royal Blue eye palette. £10.99. Ref no. 78936234.
           pg.14

Complete the missing entries in this customer order list

Item no.	Product	Colour	Price	Ref no.	Page
16	Avon Black mascara			14563259	
	Shine and Clear Powder		£3.99		9
20		Pink	£3.99		
			£3.99	45339523	7
40		Royal blue			14

INFORMATION HANDLING TEST EXERCISE 4

Study the information in the list below. The following is an extract from a Football boot embroideries sheet.

Football boot embroideries Sheet (£2 per letter per boot)

Item 1: James. Airmax 12 football boots. Size 11. 465892-06-130 Green. Both boots. £20.

Item 2: e.r.d. Puma boots. Size 9. 659846-15-650. Black. Left boot. £6

Item 3: White. Nike Firebolt football boots. Size 8. 698564-07-450. White. Both boots. £20.

Item 4: D.P. Precision Nike football boots. Size 9. 469256-15-650. Black. Both boots. £8.

Item 5: Lewis. Nike Mecurial Astro Turfs. Size 10. 259873-07-456. White. Right boot. £10.

Item 6: Marianne. Adidas Flair Astro Turfs. Size 5. 469872-18-652. Pink. Both boots. £32.

Item 7: T.J. Nike firebolt football boots. Size 10. 698564-15-450. White. Both boots. £8.

Item 8: JG8. Puma boots. Size 7. 659846-03-452. Blue. Both boots. £12.

Fill out the missing entries for this boot embroidery sheet

Item no:	Name on boots:	Boots:	Size:	Code:	Colour:	Right/Left/ Both boots:	Price:
	D.P		9	659846-15-650		both	
3		Nike firebolt	8		White		£20
5	Lewis				White	Right boot	
		Nike firebolt	10		White		
	JG8			659846-03-452			£12

INFORMATION HANDLING TEST EXERCISE 5

Study the information in the list below. The following is an extract from a 'printing on the back of football shirts' sheet.

Printing on the back of football shirts sheet

Item 1: Manchester united football shirt. Premiership. 23659779. White. Curved. David. 8.

Item 2: England football shirt. England, Away. 65987245. Navy. Straight. Jamie. 4.

Item 3: Newcastle united football shirt. Premiership. 45698523. Navy. Curved. Marianne. 10.

Item 4: England football shirt. England, Home. 65987426. White. Curved. Madison. 12

Item 5: Manchester united football shirt. Premiership. 25697523. White. Straight. Big Daddy. 50.

Item 6: Manchester united football shirt. Premiership. 46584563. White. Curved. Stephen. 16.

Item 7: England football shirt. England, Home. 46872587. White. Straight. Elizabeth. 21.

Item 8: Newcastle united football shirt. Premiership. 46987412. Navy. Curved. Oliver. 10

Fill out the missing entries from this football shirt printing sheet

Item no.	Team:	Premiership/ England:	Home/ Away:	Code:	Colour:	Straight/ Curved	Name printed:	Age printed:
2			Away	65987245			Jamie	4
	Newcastle	Premiership	-		Navy	Curved		
		Premiership	-		White		Big Daddy	
7			Home			Straight		21
4			Home	65987426			Madison	

INFORMATION HANDLING TEST EXERCISE 6

Study the information in the list below. The following is an extract from a catalogue of health and safety books.

Catalogue of health and safety books

Code 263: Health and safety: an introduction. Jackson, J. Hardcopy. Routledge: London. £29.99. ISBN 0-4569-7596

Code 264: An introduction to safety in the workplace. Harrison, A. Paperback. Palgrave: New York. £35.99. ISBN 0-7896-4236

Code 265: Safety in action. Friend, J. Hardcopy. Routledge: London. £30.00. ISBN 0-4526-8523

Code 266: Making sure your workplace is a safe place to work. Reynolds, L. Paperback. Routledge: London. £22.99. ISBN 0-3698-7412

Code 267: An introduction to rules and regulations of work environ ments. Anderson, A. Paperback. Palgrave: New York. ISBN £45.99. 0-5698-5478

Code 268: Health procedures and safety guidelines. Richards, E. Hardcopy. Routledge: London. £15.99. ISBN 0-1298-7836

Code 269: All you need to know about your workplace. Brown. E. Paper back. Routledge: London. £16.99. ISBN 0-1285-6539

Code 270: Guidelines for your work place. Powley, D. Hardcopy. Pear son Education: London. £24.99. ISBN 0-3596-0056

Code 271: The workplace: Rules and Regulations. Ericson, P. Paper back. Palgrave: New York. £16.99. ISBN 0-0069-5690

Fill out the missing entries for this boot embroidery sheet

Code:	Title:	Author:	Copy:	Publisher:	Location:	Price:	ISBN:
		Harrison, A		Palgrave		£35.99	0-7896-4236
265		Friend, J	Hardcopy		London	£30.00	
	Health procedures and safety guidelines		Hardcopy		London		
		Powley, D		Pearson Education			0-3596-0056
271	The Workplace: Rules and Regulations		Paperback		New York	£16.99	

INFORMATION HANDLING TEST EXERCISE 7

Study the information in the list below. The following is an extract from an online Dress Shopping Catalogue.

Online Dress Shopping Catalogue

Item 11: Silver Sequin Dress. Black/Silver. Size 10. Was £65.00. Now £30.00. Order no. 4652365

Item 12: Camilla Red sequinned skirt. Red/Black. Size 12. Was £30.00. Now £15.00. Order no. 4985232

Item 13: Cassandra Black fitted dress. Black. Size 8. Was £65.00. Now £45.00. Order no. 9635875

Item 14: Lilly flowered white alter neck top. White/flowery. Size 10. Was £30.00. Now £12.00. Order no. 4569852

Item 15: Roxy May Gold flare skirt. Gold/Black. Size 12. Was £50.00. Now £20.00. Order no. 9635891

Item 16: Lilly May Detailed Long sleeved black dress. Black. Size 10. Was £70.00. Now £35.00. Order no. 3596547

Item 17: Phoebe Rose Prom dress. Blue. Size 8. Was £90.00. Now £45.00 Order no. 6596325

Item 18: Sandra Sequined Silver Dress. Silver. Size 8. Was £70.00. Now £30.00. Order no. 9633687

Fill out the missing entries for this customers order form

Item no:	Product:	Colour:	Size:	Was:	Now:	Order no.
12		Red/Black	12		£15.00	
	Lilly flowered white alter neck top		10			4569852
		Gold/Black		£50.00	£20.00	9635891
17	Phoebe Rose Prom Dress		8		£45.00	
		Black		£65.00	£45.00	

INFORMATION HANDLING TEST EXERCISE 8

Study the information in the list below. The following is an extract from a catalogue from a DVD and Blu-Ray shop.

Catalogue from a DVD and Blu-Ray shop

Item 159: DVD. A walk to remember. Director: Adam Shankman. £9.99. Ref no. 3633256

Item 160: Blu-ray. Harry Potter and the Philosopher's Stone. Director: Chris Columbus. £12.99. Ref no. 5968759

Item 161: DVD. Harry Potter and the Philosopher's Stone. Director: Chris Columbus. £9.99. Ref no. 2366984

Item 162: DVD. A Nightmare on Elm Street. Director: Wes Craven. £5.99. Ref no. 4568798

Item 163: DVD. Titanic. Director: James Cameron. £8.99. Ref no. 4698677

Item 164: Blu-ray. Titanic. Director: James Cameron. £12.99. Ref no. 4566598

Item 165: DVD. War of the Worlds. Director: Steven Spielberg. £10.99. Ref no. 3652206

Item 166: Blu-ray. War of the Worlds. Director: Steven Spielberg. £15.99. Ref no. 6986326

Fill out the missing entries for this customers order list

Item no:	DVD/ Blu-ray	Film title:	Director:	Price:	Ref no:
160			Chris Columbus	£12.99	5968759
	DVD		Chris Columbus		2366984
	DVD	Titanic		£8.99	
166			Steven Spielberg		

INFORMATION HANDLING TEST EXERCISE 9

Study the information in the list below. The following is an extract from a men's fashion clothing website.

Men's fashion clothing website

Code 125: Men's tailor made fitted jacket. Black. Size small. £25.99. Ref no. 46356978

Code 126: Boy's tailor made fitted jacket. Black. Size 9-10. £12.99. Ref no. 23659865

Code 127: Boy's tailor made fitted jacket. Brown. Size 9-10. £12.99. Ref no. 3698563

Code 128: Hand-stitched chequered jumper. Blue/Black. Size M. £18.99. Ref no. 45698536

Code 129: Men's skinny jeans. Black. Size 32 waist. £25.99. Ref no. 45236635

Code 130: Men's skinny jeans. Navy. Size 34 waist. £25.99. Ref no. 41255325

Code 131: Nike t-shirt. White/Navy. Size M. £10.99. Ref no. 12696363

Code 132: Adidas t-shirt. White/Black. Size S. £8.99. Ref no. 43696589

Code 133: Woolly round neck jumper. Burgundy. Size M. £10.99. Ref no. 63569853

Fill out the missing entries for this customers order form

Item no:	Product:	Colour:	Size:	Price:	Ref no:
	Boy's tailor made fitted jacket		9-10		3698563
126		Black	9-10		
			M	£18.99	45698536
133		Burgundy		£10.99	63569853
		Navy	Size 34 waist		41255325

INFORMATION HANDLING TEST EXERCISE 10

Study the information in the list below. The following is an extract from catalogue items for a carpet store.

Catalogue items for a carpet store

Item 120: Extra comfort and padded carpet. Black/Silver. Size 12x4. £29.99. Delivery date: 13/05/2014

Item 121: Leopard print rug. Leopard print. Size 3x4. £16.99. Delivery date: 10/05/2014

Item 122: Extra fitted carpet and skirting. Burgundy. Size 25x20. £38.99 Delivery date: 17/05/2014

Item 123: Persian rug. Black. Size 10x8. £16.99. Delivery date: 21/05/2014

Item 124: Persian rug. Brown. Size 12x8. £22.99. Delivery date: 22/05/2014

Item 125: Extra comfort and padded carpet. Cream. Size 20x16. £46.99. Delivery date: 12/05/2014

Item 126: Leopard print rug. Leopard print. Size 10x8. £32.99. Delivery date: 10/05/2014

Item 127: Extra fitted carpet, skirting and underlay. Size 8x5. £120.00. Delivery date: 12/05/2014

Fill out the missing entries for this customers order list

Item no:	Product:	Colour:	Size:	Price:	Delivery date:
	Extra comfort and padded carpet		Size 12x4		13/05/2014
122		Burgundy	Size 25x20		
	Persian rug	Black		£16.99	
		Brown	Size 12x8	£22.99	

ANSWERS TO INFORMATION HANDLING INTERMEDIATE (SECTION 2)

ANSWERS TO INFORMATION HANDLING TEST EXERCISE 1

£26.99

Lewis T

ISBN 0-9647-2535

Code 130

Theories of youth culture

Davidson, H

£12.99

Understanding contemporary youth

Hardback

Code 123

Blackman, R

Paperback

ISBN 0-3658-4532

£18.99

Introduction to youth culture

ISBN 0-4698-6983

ANSWERS TO INFORMATION HANDLING TEST EXERCISE 2

Sophie May Backless Dress

Size 10.

£45.00

Ref no: 2569873

Code 112
Aqua
Size 12
Ref no. 4258793

Rosie Jane Bodycon Dress
Pink
£10.00

Code 117
Size 10
£9.99
Ref no. 1236852

Code 118
Juliette swirl Bodycon dress
Green
Size 12

ANSWERS TO INFORMATION HANDLING TEST EXERCISE 3

Black
£5.99
pg. 5

Item 25
Translucent
Ref no. 56985326

Shimmery Lip gloss
Ref no. 45339522
pg. 7

Item 21

Shimmery Lip gloss

Clear

Shimmery Royal Blue eye palette

£10.99

Ref no. 78936234

ANSWERS TO INFORMATION HANDLING TEST EXERCISE 4

Item 4

Precision Nike football boots

Black

£8

White

698564-07-450

Both boots

Nike Mecurial Astro Turfs

Size 10

259873-07-456

£10

Item 7

T.J

698564-15-450

Both boots

£8

Item 8

Puma boots
Size 7
Blue
Both boots

ANSWERS TO INFORMATION HANDLING TEST EXERCISE 5

England football shirt
England
Navy
Straight

Item 3
45698523
Marianne
10

Item 5
Manchester united football shirt
25697523
Straight
50

England football shirt
England
46872587
White
Elizabeth

England football shirt
England
White
Curved
12

ANSWERS TO INFORMATION HANDLING TEST EXERCISE 6

Code 264

An introduction to safety in the workplace

Paperback

New York

Safety in action

Routledge

ISBN 0-4526-8523

Code 268

Richards, E

Routledge

£15.99

ISBN 0-1298-7836

Code 270

Guidelines for your work place

Hardcopy

London

£24.99

Ericson, P

Palgrave

ISBN 0-0069-5690

ANSWERS TO INFORMATION HANDLING TEST EXERCISE 7

Camilla Red sequinned skirt

Was £30.00

Order no. 4985232

Item 14
White/flowery
Was £30.00
Now £12.00

Item 15
Roxy May Gold flare skirt
Size 12

Blue
Was £90.00
Order no. 6596325

Item 13
Cassandra Black fitted dress
Size 8
Order no. 9635875

ANSWERS TO INFORMATION HANDLING TEST EXERCISE 8

Blu-ray
Harry Potter and the Philosopher's Stone.

Item 161
Harry Potter and the Philosopher's Stone
£9.99

Item 163
Director: James Cameron
Ref no. 4698677

Blu-ray
War of the Worlds
£15.99.
Ref no. 6986326

ANSWERS TO INFORMATION HANDLING TEST EXERCISE 9

Code 127
Brown
£12.99

Boy's tailor made fitted jacket
£12.99
Ref no. 23659865

Code 128
Hand-stitched chequered jumper.
Blue/Black

Woolly round neck jumper
Size M

Code 130
Men's skinny jeans
£25.99

ANSWERS TO INFORMATION HANDLING TEST EXERCISE 10

Item 120
Black/Silver
£29.99

Extra fitted carpet and skirting
£38.99.
Delivery date: 17/05/2014

Item 123
Size 10x8
Delivery date: 21/05/2014

Item 124
Persian rug
Delivery date: 22/05/2014

ADVANCED

SECTION 1

PLEASE NOTE:

For this section, the questions are NOT an exact replica of the questions in your Scottish Police exam. Instead, they can be used to better your understanding and skills in regards to handling information.

Study the following table and answer questions 1 to 5.

Based on 100 students and their marks in English, Maths and Science examinations.

Subject	Marks out of 40			
	30 and above	20 and above	10 and above	0 and above
English	19	52	91	100
Maths	13	36	90	100
Science	11	42	87	100
AVERAGE	11	43	89	100

Question 1

If at least 50% in their examination is needed to go on to higher education, how many students in Maths can go on to higher education?

A	B	C	D	E
49	13	36	19	27

Question 2

What is the percentage of students who achieved marks of 20 or above in their English exam?

A	B	C	D	E
36%	41%	56%	52%	48%

Question 3

What is the difference between the number of students who achieved 30 or above in English and the number of students who achieved 20 and above in Science?

A	B	C	D	E
23	25	27	31	19

Question 4

How many people scored 10 or above but below 20, in their Maths exam?

A	B	C	D	E
43	57	90	13	54

Question 5

What subject had the highest number of students who scored below 10?

A	B	C	D	E
English	Maths	Science	All the same	English and Maths

Study the following table and answer the questions 6 to 10.

Employees in departments of a company

Department	January	February	March	April	May	June
Marketing	21	24	17	15	23	27
Admin	18	11	15	13	13	18
Sales	21	22	29	31	28	24
IT	19	13	17	18	22	25

Question 6

How many employees are there in May?

A	B	C	D	E
71	78	83	86	89

Question 7

What was the average number of employees for February, across all departments?

A	B	C	D	E
9.75	17.5	11.5	13	19.75

Question 8

What was the average number of Admin employees over the 6 month period? To the nearest whole number.

A	B	C	D	E
11	17	15	21	24

Question 9

What was the largest number of people employed at one given time? (I.e. in any month, in any department).

A	B	C	D	E
29	31	27	35	26

Question 10

What is the difference between the total number of employees in Marketing, and the total number of employees in Sales, across the six month period?

A	B	C	D	E
21	26	31	28	35

Study the following chart and answer the questions 11 to 15.

A pie chart representing the number of crimes in a one month period.

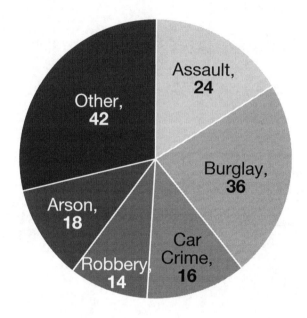

Question 11

What percentage of the total number of crimes were assault – related?

A	B	C	D	E
9%	36%	16%	6%	13%

Question 12

How many crimes are there in total?

A	B	C	D	E
95	100	125	150	175

Question 13

What was the average number of crimes across the one month period?

A	B	C	D	E
25	50	15	20	45

Question 14

Work out the difference between the lowest occurring type of crime, and the highest occurring type of crime.

A	B	C	D	E
21	28	32	16	26

Question 15

What percentage of the total number of crimes were burglary and arson-related?

A	B	C	D	E
21%	55%	61%	42%	36%

Study the following table and answer the questions 16 to 20.

BMW sales

Country	Jan	Feb	Mar	April	May	June	Total
UK	21	28	15	35	31	20	150
Germany	45	48	52	36	41	40	262
France	32	36	33	28	20	31	180
Brazil	42	41	37	32	35	28	215
Spain	22	26	17	30	24	22	141
Italy	33	35	38	28	29	38	201
Total	195	214	192	189	180	179	1149

The above table shows the sales across 6 countries for the model BMW for a 6 month period. The BMW's are imported to each country from a main dealer.

Question 16

What percentage of the overall total was sold in April?

A	B	C	D	E
17.8%	17.2%	18.9%	16.4%	21.6%

Question 17

What percentage of the overall total sales were BMW's sold to the French importer?

A	B	C	D	E
15.6%	18.2%	18.9%	25.6%	24.5%

Question 18

What percentage of total imports is accounted for by the two smallest importers?

A	B	C	D	E
35.6%	25.3%	22.6%	28.1%	29.1%

Question 19

What is the average number of units per month imported to Brazil over the first 4 months of the year?

A	B	C	D	E
28	24	32	38	40

Question 20

What month saw the biggest increase in total sales from the previous month?

A	B	C	D	E
January	February	March	April	May

ANSWERS TO INFORMATION HANDLING ADVANCED (SECTION 1)

Q1. C = 36

EXPLANATION = 50% of 40 = 20. Number of students who scored 20 and above in Maths = 36.

Q2. D = 52%

EXPLANATION = 100 students, 52 students achieved marks of 20 or above = 52%.

Q3. A = 23

EXPLANATION = Number of students with 30 or above in English = 19. Students with 20 or above in Science = 42. So 42 - 19 = 23.

Q4. E = 54

EXPLANATION = looking at the Maths row, you need to work out how many people scored 10 or above (90) but below 20. 36 of the the 90 people scored 20 or above, therefore the number of people who scored 10 or above but below 20 is = 90 – 36 = 54.

Q5. C = Science

EXPLANATION = scores of 10 or below = English = 9, Maths = 10, Science = 13.

Q6. D = 86

EXPLANATION = 23 + 13 + 28 + 22 = 86.

Q7. B = 17.5

EXPLANATION = 24 + 11 + 22 + 13 = 70

70 ÷ 4 = 17.5.

Q8. C = 15

EXPLANATION = 18 + 11 + 15 + 13 + 13 + 18 = 88

88 ÷ 6 = 14.6. To the nearest whole number = 15.

Q9. B = 31

EXPLANATION = the largest number of people employed at any given time occurred in April, and that was for the department of Sales.

Q10. D = 28

EXPLANATION = Marketing 21 + 24 + 17 + 15 + 23 + 27 = 127. Sales 21 + 22 + 29 + 31 + 28 + 24 = 155.
155 – 127 = 28.

Q11. C = 16%

EXPLANATION = 24 ÷ 150 x 100 = 16%.

Q12. D = 150

EXPLANATION = 42 + 18 + 14 + 16 + 36 + 24 = 150.

Q13. A = 25

EXPLANATION = 150 ÷ 6 = 25.

Q14. B = 28

EXPLANATION = 42 – 14 = 28.

Q15. E = 36%

EXPLANATION = 36 + 18 = 54
54 ÷ 150 x 100 = 36%.

Q16. D = 16.4%

EXPLANATION = to work out the percentage overall total that was sold in April, divide how many BMW's were sold in April (189) by the total (1149) and then multiply it by 100. (189 ÷ 1149 x 100 = 16.4%).

Q17. A = 15.6%

EXPLANTATION = to work out the percentage overall total that was sold to France, divide how many BMW's were sold to France (180) by the total (1149) and then multiply it by 100. (180 ÷ 1149 x 100 = 15.6%).

Q18. B = 25.3%

EXPLANTATION = to work out the percentage overall for imports accounted by the two smallest importers, divide how many BMW's were sold from the two smallest importers (UK and France = 150 + 141 = 291) by the total (1149) and then multiply it by 100. (291 ÷ 1149 x 100 = 25.3%).

Q19. D = 38

EXPLANTATION = to work out the average number of units per month imported to Brazil over the first 4 months of the year, you add up the first 4 amounts (Jan-April) and then divide it by how many numbers there are (4). So, (42 + 41 + 37 + 32 = 152 ÷ 4 = 38).

Q20. B = February

EXPLANATION = to work out the biggest increase in total sales from the previous month, you work out the difference between the totals for each of the month. Between January and February, there was an increase by 19. None of the other months have a bigger increase and therefore February is the correct answer.

ADVANCED

SECTION 2

PLEASE NOTE:

For this section, the questions are NOT an exact replica
of the questions in your Scottish Police exam. Instead,
they can be used to better your understanding and
skills in regards to handling information.

Study the below table and answer the question 1 to 5.

The table shows imports for three types of wood over a 6 month period.

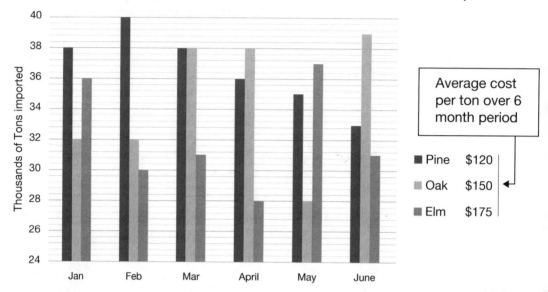

Question 1

What was the difference in thousands of tons between oak wood and elm wood imports in the first 3 months of the year?

A	B	C	D	E
2,000	5,000	4,000	9,000	11,000

Question 2

What was the total, in thousands of tons, for pine across the six month period?

A	B	C	D	E
210,000	180,000	195,000	205,000	220,000

Question 3

What was the total value of oak wood ($) imported over the 6 month period?

A	B	C	D	E
31,050	42,550	32,500	30,050	36,550

Question 4

Which month showed the largest total decrease in imports over the previous month?

A	B	C	D	E
March	January	June	February	April

Question 5

What was the average of elm wood imported over the 6 month period?

A	B	C	D	E
33.1	32.2	35.5	31	40.5

Study the following table and answer the questions 6 to 10.

The table shows the number of English papers published by top UK universities over a six year period.

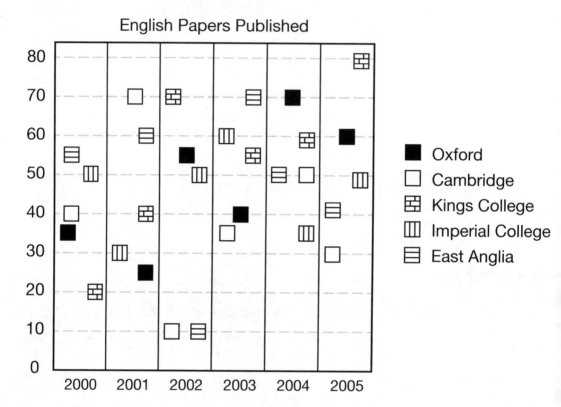

English Papers Published

■ Oxford
□ Cambridge
▦ Kings College
▥ Imperial College
▤ East Anglia

Question 6

How many papers did Oxford publish altogether?

A	B	C	D	E
275	215	325	285	260

Question 7

In what year did researchers at Cambridge publish most papers?

A	B	C	D	E
2000	2001	2002	2003	2004

Question 8

How many papers were published by Imperial College in 2004?

A	B	C	D	E
70	60	55	35	50

Question 9

In what year did East Anglia College publish the lowest number of papers?

A	B	C	D	E
2001	2002	2003	2004	2005

Question 10

How many papers were published by Cambridge University over the six year period?

A	B	C	D	E
275	285	235	245	280

Study the following table and answer questions 11 to 15.

Determine the correct code using the table provided. Orders are coded as follows: ORDER – COST – SHIPPING METHOD.

ORDER	CODE	COST	CODE	SHIPPING METHOD	CODE
Nails	789	Less than $100	RR	UPS	20
Screws	654	$100-$250	SS	Emery Worldwide	30
Paint	123	$251-$350	TT	DHL	40
Saw	912	$351-$450	UU	Federal Express	50
Wood	829	$451-$550	VV	Airborne Express	60
Telephone	296	$551-$650	WW	Standard Mail	70
Clock	328	$651-$750	XX	Customer Walk-In	80

Question 11

What would be the code for an order of paint that cost $120.75 and shipped by standard mail?

A – 789-TT-70

B – 829-SS-70

C – 123-SS-70

D – 123-SS-80

Answer [   ]

Question 12

The code 829-UU-50 is CORRECT for an order of?

A – Wood costing $375.50 and shipped via federal express
B – Paint costing $375.50 and shipped via federal express
C – Wood costing $120.75 and shipped via airborne mail
D – Paint costing $375.25 and shipped via airborne mail

Answer

Question 13

An order of screws arrived that cost $125.50. If the order is shipped via DHL, it would be coded?

A – 654-SS-40
B – 654-TT-40
C – 789-SS-40
D – 789-TT-50

Answer

Question 14

An order of saws costing $514.25 shipped via Emery Worldwide was coded 829-WW-30 in error. Of the following, which is the CORRECT code for this order?

A – 912-WW-30

B – 912-VV-30

C – 123-XX-50

D – 296-VV-40

Answer

Question 15

An order of clocks costing $325.00 was sold to a walk-in customer. What is the CORRECT code for this transaction?

A – 296-RR-20

B – 654-RR-50

C – 328-SS-70

D – 328-TT-80

Answer

Study the following table and answer the questions 16 to 20.

Determine the correct training code based on the information provided in the table. Training instruction provided to employees is coded as: INSTRUCTOR – TRAINING – TRAINING SITE – DATE.

INSTRUCTOR	CODE	TRAINING	CODE	TRAINING SITE	CODE	DATE	CODE
Walker	222	First Aid	H	Main Library	353	June 3	AAA
Brown	555	Contracting	J	Ramsay Campus	215	June 4	BBB
Powley	777	Budgeting	B	Arboretum	795	June 8	CCC
Wells	888	Data Analysis	T	Powell Office	635	August 7	DDD
White	999	Writing	I	Hyde Garage	328	August 11	EEE
Thompson	111	Computers	N	Wester Hall	701	August 18	FFF
Thomas	333	Mechanics	R	Public Works	008	August 23	GGG

Question 16

The code 777-T-215-CCC is CORRECT for?

A – Contracting training taught by Thompson at the Main Library on August 7th

B – Contracting training taught by Powley at the Ramsay Campus on June 8th.

C – Data analysis training taught by Powley at the Ramsay Campus on June 8th.

D – Contracting training taught by Thomas at the Powell Office on August 18th.

Answer

Question 17

Walker wants to conduct writing training at the Powell Office. If the department schedules the training for the 23rd August, the code would be?

A – 555-I-328-EEE

B – 222-I-635-GGG

C – 111-I-635-GGG

D – 111-T-795-DDD

Answer

Question 18

Wells received her training schedule and saw the code 888-H-353-CCC. She notified her supervisor that the training needed to be moved to Wester Hall. The training was subsequently recoded?

A – 888-H-701-CCC

B – 555-H-701-CCC

C – 999-B-701-AAA

D – 333-T-635-FFF

Answer

Question 19

White was scheduled to conduct Mechanical training at Hyde Garage on June 4th, but Thomas had to substitute at the last minute. The revised code for the training is?

A – 333-J-795-CCC

B – 999-R-328-BBB

C – 333-R-328-BBB

D – 111-N-795-DDD

Answer [   ]

Question 20

The code 555-B-353-FFF is CORRECT for?

A – Budgeting training taught by Brown at the Main Library on August 18th.

B – Contracting training taught by Wells at the Main Library on August 7th.

C – Budgeting training taught by Wells at the Main Library on August 7th.

D – Contracting training taught by Brown at the Main Library on August 18th.

Answer [   ]

ANSWERS TO INFORMATION HANDLING ADVANCED (SECTION 2)

Q1. B

EXPLANATION = to work out the difference, add up the first 3 months for Oak (32 + 32 + 38 = 102). Add up the first 3 months for Elm (36 + 30 + 31 = 97). So, the difference between Oak and Elm = 5 (thousands).

Q2. E

EXPLANATION = 38 + 40 + 38 + 36 + 35 + 33 = 220 (220,000)

Q3. A

EXPLANATION = (32 + 32 + 38 + 38 + 28 + 39 = 207 x 150 = 31,050).

Q4. E

EXPLANATION = the highest decrease was between March and April, March's total = 107, April's total = 102. The difference is 5, no other months have a higher decreased number.

Q5. B

EXPLANATION =193 ÷ 6 = 32.166

Q6. D

EXPLANATION = the number of papers published by Oxford university, across the six month period = 35 + 25 + 55 + 40 + 70 + 60 = 285

Q7. B

EXPLANATION = Cambridge published 70 papers in the year 2001. This was the highest record for them across the six year period.

Q8. D

EXPLANATION = In 2004, Imperial College published 35 papers.

Q9. B

EXPLANATION = East Anglia College only published 10 papers in the year 2002. This was the lowest number of papers published by this institution across the six year period.

Q10. C

EXPLANATION = Overall, Cambridge University published 235 papers across the six year period.

Q11. C

EXPLANATION = the correct answer is C. The code for paint (123) costing $120.75 (SS) and shipped by standard mail (70).

Q12. A

EXPLANATION = the correct answer is A. The code 829-UU-50 is correct for wood (829) costing $375.50 (UU) and shipped via federal express (50).

Q13. A

EXPLANATION = the correct answer is A. The entry would be coded as 654 (screws), SS (costing $125.50) and 40 (shipped via DHL).

Q14. B

EXPLANATION = the correct answer is B. The order should have been coded as 912 (saws), VV (costing $514.25), 30 (shipped via Emery Worldwide).

Q15. D

EXPLANATION = the correct answer is D. The most appropriate code for the transaction would be 328 (clocks), TT (costing $325) 80 (via customer walk-in).

Q16. C

EXPLANATION = The correct answer is C. The code 777-T-215-CCC would signify that Powley (777) taught Data analysis Training (T) at the Ramsay Campus (215) on June 8th (CCC).

Q17. B

EXPLANATION = The correct answer is B. The code for this training would be 222 (Walker) –I (Writing) –635 (Powell Office) –GGG (August 23rd).

Q18. A

EXPLANATION = The correct answer is A. The training would be recoded as 888 (Wells) –H (First Aid) –701 (Wester Hall) –CCC (June 8th).

Q19. C

EXPLANATION = The correct answer is C. The revised code for the training would be 333 (Thomas) –R (Mechanics) –328 (Hyde Garage) –BBB (June 4th).

Q20. A

EXPLANATION = The correct answer is A. This code is correct for Budgeting training (B) conducted by Brown (555) at the Main Library (353) on August 18th (FFF).

A FEW FINAL WORDS

You have now reached the end of the testing guide and no doubt you will be ready to take the INFORMATION HANDLING test element of the Scottish Police Test.

The majority of candidates who pass the police officer selection process have a number of common attributes. These are as follows:

1. They believe in themselves.

The first factor is self-belief. Regardless of what anyone tells you, you can become a police officer. Just like any job of this nature, you have to be prepared to work hard in order to be successful. Make sure you have the self-belief to pass the selection process and fill your mind with positive thoughts.

2. They prepare fully.

The second factor is preparation. Those people who achieve in life prepare fully for every eventuality and that is what you must do when you apply to become a police officer. Work very hard and especially concentrate on your weak areas.

3. They persevere.

Perseverance is a fantastic word. Everybody comes across obstacles or setbacks in their life, but it is what you do about those setbacks that is important. If you fail at something, then ask yourself 'why' you have failed. This will allow you to improve for next time and if you keep improving and trying, success will eventually follow. Apply this same method of thinking when you apply to become a police officer.

4. They are self-motivated.

How much do you want this job? Do you want it, or do you *really* want it?

When you apply to join the police you should want it more than anything in the world. Your levels of self-motivation will shine through on your application and during your interview. For the weeks and months leading up to the police officer selection process, be motivated as best you can and always keep your fitness levels up as this will serve to increase your levels of motivation.

Work hard, stay focused and be what you want…

The How2become Team

P.S. Don't forget, you can get FREE access to more tests online at:

www.PsychometricTestsOnline.co.uk

how2become

Attend a 1 Day Police Officer Training Course at:

www.PoliceCourse.co.uk

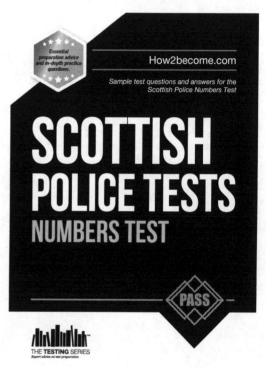